JOHNNY UNITAS
AND THE LONG PASS

JOHNNY UNITAS
AND THE LONG PASS

by Julian May

Published by Crestwood House, Inc., Mankato, Minnesota 56001. Published simultaneously in Canada by J. M. Dent and Sons, Ltd. Library of Congress Catalog Card Number: 72-77302. Standard Book Number: 87191-200-7. Text copyright © 1972 by Julian May Dikty. Illustrations copyright © 1972 by Crestwood House, Inc. All rights reserved. No part of this book may be reproduced in any form without written permission from the publisher, except for brief passages included in a review. Printed in the United States of America.

Designed by William Dichtl

Crestwood House, Inc., Mankato, Minn. 56001

PHOTOGRAPHIC CREDITS

Courier-Journal Louisville Times: 9, 15; National Football League: 2, 17, 20 (Malcolm W. Emmons), 25 (Malcolm W. Emmons), 28 (Vernon J. Brever), 31, 34, 39 (Malcolm W. Emmons), 42, 44; United Press International: 6, 10, 16, 18, 19, 21, 22, 23, 24, 27, 30, 32, 36, 37, 40, 41, 45, 47; University of Louisville: 12, 13; Wide World Photos: 26, 35.
Cover: National Football League.

JOHNNY UNITAS
AND THE LONG PASS

He was a skinny boy, but tall, with great big hands. His family lived in Pittsburgh. His father was dead, so he helped with the family's coal delivery business. He could earn 75 cents a ton shoveling coal into people's basement bins.

Young Johnny Unitas had always wanted to play pro football. He knew he would have to go to college, since almost every pro came from college team ranks.

But the Unitas family was poor. The only way Johnny could go to college was with an athletic scholarship. College scouts looked the boy over. He visited Notre Dame and Indiana University.

And they turned him down. "Too skinny," the coaches said.

Deep concentration shows on Johnny's face as he practices at the University of Louisville.

His steady girl friend, Dorothy Hoelle, tried to cheer him up. "You'll find a school, Johnny," she said.

Finally, when he had just about given up, the University of Louisville, in Kentucky, offered him a scholarship.

Johnny practiced hard. But like the other freshman players, he spent most of his time on the bench. Louisville lost three out of the first four games.

Johnny warms up his arm.

Frank Camp, head football coach at the University of Louisville, saw that young Johnny Unitas had the makings of a champion quarterback.

Coach Frank Camp said, "Next week we play St. Bonaventure in New York. They've got a tough team. I've decided to start Johnny as quarterback."

Johnny said, "I'll give it my best, Coach."

On the day of the game, a light rain was falling. At first, Johnny was tense and excited.

"Easy does it, Johnny," said Coach Camp. "You're trying too hard. Take a rest, and I'll let you try again in the second half."

The St. Bonaventure team wasn't bothered by the rain. At the end of the half the score was 19-0 in the Bonnies' favor.

Then Johnny tried again. He completed eleven straight passes—three for touchdowns. They converted each time, and they were ahead, 21-19.

A last-period field goal gave the Bonnies three points. The Louisville Cardinals lost, 22-21. But when they got home, a happy crowd greeted them like winners. And Coach Camp said:

"For the rest of the season, my quarterback is going to be Johnny Unitas."

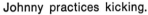

Johnny practices kicking.

Johnny's nerves cooled off. He was loose and in control. Helped by his great passing, Louisville won the next game, 26-2.

The seventh game put them up against Houston. The Texans were expected to win, but the surprising Cardinals fought them to a 21-21 tie in the last quarter.

It was fourth down and two yards to go on the Houston 40-yard line.

In the huddle, a powerful Louisville fullback said, "Give me the ball, Johnny. I'll get the two yards."

Johnny said, "When I want you to take it, I'll let you know."

Houston was expecting a rush. But Johnny dropped back and passed to one of his ends for a touchdown.

"You've got to keep 'em guessing," Johnny said to the team. "And you've got to remember that the quarterback calls the shots—even when he's a freshman!"

Time began to run out. Houston caught the Cardinals' defense by surprise, and quick-kicked the ball to Louisville's 4-yard line. Johnny sent his halfback crashing into the line twice, but they only picked up three yards.

It was time for another "keep 'em guessing" play. Johnny fell back into his own end zone, faking and sidestepping the amazed Houston defense. He let go a 40-yard pass to end Babe Ray, who raced 60 yards for another touchdown.

Louisville won that game, and the next two as well. The underdog Cardinals finished the 1951 season winning five out of nine.

With football over, Johnny worked harder than ever on his studies. Friendly teachers helped him. He kept a C average and his scholarship was safe.

But other players on the team weren't so lucky. A new president came to Louisville, and he canceled the scholarships of 15 players with low grades. All of a sudden, almost half the team was gone!

A coach from a Big Ten college came to Johnny and tried to get him to transfer. But Johnny stayed loyal to the school that had given him a chance when nobody else wanted him.

Johnny and his wife, Dorothy, head out for a drive.

He stayed at Louisville and did his best, while the crippled team had three losing seasons in a row.

At the start of his senior year, in 1954, he broke his ankle in a pre-season scrimmage. But he played anyhow. He was just about all the team had.

Throughout college, his high-school sweetheart, Dorothy, had remained his closest friend. Midway into an awful 1954 season, he and Dorothy were married. He limped down the aisle smiling broadly. He wasn't alone any more!

Before long, his college football days came to an end. He graduated from Louisville and faced the big challenge—breaking into the National Football League.

The Pittsburgh Steelers took him as a ninth-round draft choice. He reported to their New York training camp in the fall of 1955.

But a great disappointment was in store for him. None of the coaches seemed too happy with his quarterbacking. He was blitzed again and again by defensive men before he could pass or make the handoff. He fumbled and made other mistakes. He forgot signals.

The Steelers finally let Johnny go. Broke and discouraged, he hitchhiked back home to Pittsburgh, to Dorothy, and to their newborn baby daughter.

It was too late to sign up with another team that year. He got a job as a pile driver with a building firm. To keep in shape, he played semipro football in the Greater Pittsburgh League.

His team, the Bloomfield Rams, was a real sandlot club. They rarely used the fancy plays of college teams. For the Rams, football was a rough and tumble affair that often ended with a fist fight. But Johnny led them to the league championship.

And for his efforts, he was paid six dollars a game. Win or lose.

Many fans felt Johnny was good enough for pro football. They sent cards and newspaper clippings to the coaches of several pro teams. And Coach Camp of Louisville also spoke about his great quarterback to friends in the professional league.

One day in February, 1956, Johnny got a phone call. It was the manager of the Baltimore Colts. He wanted Johnny to come and work out for Coach Weeb Ewbank.

Johnny looked at his wife. Another baby was on the way. "Should I take a chance?" he asked. "You say the word, and I'll stick to my steady job."

Dorothy said, "John Unitas, you go and show them."

He went. He showed them, and they snapped him up.

Coach Weeb Ewbank of the Baltimore Colts poses with Johnny Unitas.

The Colts needed Johnny. They had ranked only fourth during 1955, and they had only one other quarterback, George Shaw. Shaw played a great first game against the Chicago Bears. The Colts won. And Johnny stayed on the bench.

He spent the next two games on the sidelines, too, watching his team lose. Then it was time to meet the Bears again. The Chicago defense made Shaw their target for the day. Early in the second quarter they got him. The Colt quarterback was buried under a big pileup of Bear linemen. His knee was injured badly.

Coach Ewbank sent in the only other quarterback he had: Number 19, Johnny Unitas.

Warming the bench, Johnny longs to get into action.

On a fake pass play, Johnny bursts through the Chicago Bears' line.

The game won, the quarterback gets a free ride to the locker-room from admiring team-mates. Holding Johnny up after a 1959 triumph are Colt guard Steve Myhra and Carl Taseff.

The score was 20-14 in the Bears' favor. Johnny and the Colts didn't do much during the rest of the first half. In the third quarter, Colt back Carl Taseff carried the ball 96 yards for a touchdown. With the extra point, the Colts went ahead, 21-20.

Johnny tried hard during his first pro game. But he hadn't had a chance to work with the first-string team. His handoffs were terrible. Two fumbles brought the Bears two touchdowns. A pass interception gave them another. And so it went, with the Colts finally losing 58-27. Johnny felt it was mostly his fault.

Coach Ewbank had Johnny practice like a demon the next week. He did endless handoffs to cure the fumbles. He practiced passing to the Colts' prime receivers, Lenny Moore, Jim Mutscheller, and Raymond Berry. He worked with the team, and they worked with him.

When Sunday came, they met the Green Bay Packers and won, 28-21.

After the game, Johnny said, "The best thing I did was keep handing the ball to Lenny Moore!"

Moore had gained 185 yards in that game, including touchdown runs of 72 and 79 yards.

The coach said, "You did all right too, Johnny."

But he hired another quarterback—just in case.

Lenny Moore, the Colts' great running back, makes a 20-yard gain.

Fullback Alan Ameche was famous for blasting through the opponent's defense.

The next game, against the Cleveland Browns, was a grudge fight. The Browns were favored to win. But Johnny ran when they expected him to pass, taking the ball to the one-yard line. His huge fullback, Alan "the Horse" Ameche, went over for a touchdown.

When the Browns lay in wait for another pass, Johnny made a pitchout to Lenny Moore. Moore went 73 yards to score. Then Johnny switched to short passes. Colt backs took the ball down the field in play after play. The game ended in an upset: Colts 21, Browns 7.

The new sub quarterback stayed on the bench. The coach was satisfied to stick with Johnny. At the end of the 1956 season, the sandlot rookie finished as number-six quarterback in the league. The team was still in fourth place—but Johnny had only begun to show what he could do.

During 1957 he became famous for taking chances out on the field. Often enough, his gambles paid off. The rest of the team was in fine shape. The receivers were fast, smart, and sticky-fingered. Johnny became famous for his long "bomb" pass. He could throw with accuracy for about 70 yards.

Another Johnny Unitas pass play begins.

There were broken hearts in Baltimore during 1957. The team ended with a 7-5-0 record, third in the league. Four of their five defeats had occurred in the last minute of play.

"Just wait until next year!" said Weeb Ewbank.

For the Unitas family, the first two years of Johnny's pro career were a time of dreams come true. Johnny won the Jim Thorpe Trophy for outstanding NFL player.

And at last they were no longer poor. Johnny, Dorothy and the children now had a nice home. Even though he was a famous quarterback, Johnny always seemed to have time to throw the ball for awhile with the neighborhood kids.

Out on the gridiron, Johnny was like a commanding general. But at home, he was quiet, almost shy. His idea of fun was relaxing with his family.

Dorothy and Johnny sit for a family portrait with their four children. From left to right: Christopher, 5 days; Janice, 3; John Jr., 4; Robert, 18 months.

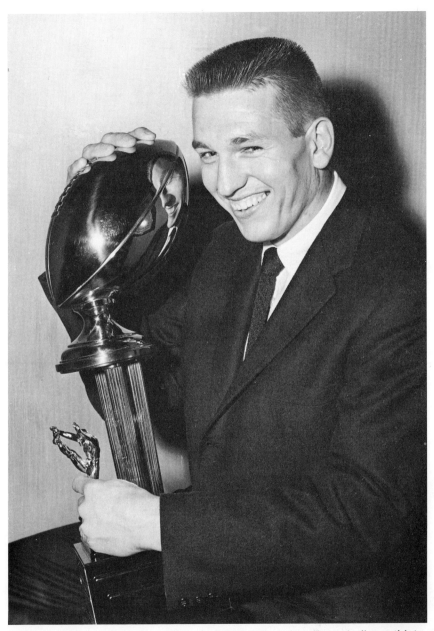

The Jim Thorpe Trophy, named for the famed American Indian athlete, went to Johnny Unitas in 1957. He was honored as most valuable player in the NFL.

The galloping Colts won their first five games in 1958. Then they played Green Bay. In the third quarter, the Colts were leading, 21-0. Johnny had to run with the ball himself when no receivers were open. The Packer defense fell on top of him. When the pileup was removed, there Johnny lay—with three broken ribs.

George Shaw finished the game and Johnny went to the hospital. Baltimore fans were happy with the 56-0 victory. But they were worried when it seemed their star quarterback would be out for the rest of the season.

Next weekend, Johnny watched the game on television. The Colts lost.

A Green Bay defender rushes at Johnny.

Rumors went around town that Johnny might not be back that season. But next Sunday he was there, sitting on the bench as his team faced the Chicago Bears. He wore aluminum and foam-rubber "armor" over his cracked ribs. He announced he was ready to go in if they needed him.

Perhaps just having him sit there as a mascot was enough. The Colts whipped Chicago, 17-0.

Next week, facing the Los Angeles Rams, the Colts really needed Johnny. He played, and the Rams went all-out to blitz him. The Colts won, 34-7. But not before Johnny had been forced to "eat" the ball a dozen times to keep it out of the hands of the red-doggers.

His injuries hurt a lot. But he never said a word.

Trainer Ed Block adjusts Johnny's protective "armor" that guards his cracked ribs.

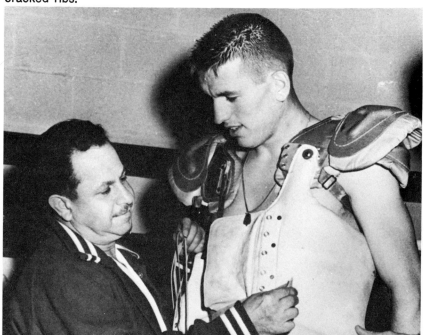

Sitting on the bench, Johnny may be trying to "think" the Colts to victory.

The Colts wound up that 1958 season with a record of nine and three, topping the Eastern Conference.

The championship game was played against the four-time champion New York Giants. It was destined to become known as "the greatest football game ever played"—the first overtime game in the history of the NFL.

For the first 58 minutes, the two teams fought a hard game. The score was Giants 17, Colts 14. Then the Colts took possession on their own 14-yard line.

Two minutes remained.

Hugging the ball, Johnny charges forward for a small gain during the 1958 championship game against the New York Giants. Halfback Carl Karilivacz (21) and linebacker Sam Huff (70) are bowled out of the way.

Johnny *(left)* and Raymond Berry size up the opposition.

There was no time for huddles as the Colts tried to beat the clock. Johnny fired pass after pass to his favorite receiver, end Raymond Berry.

Berry was a slim man, so near-sighted that he had to wear large contact lenses on the field. The handicap did not stop him from becoming all-time top pass receiver.

Three beautiful catches by Berry took the Colts 73 yards. In the last seconds, Steve Myhra kicked a tying field goal. The fans screeched and danced like madmen.

Now the Colts and Giants faced a "sudden death" overtime period. The first team to score would win.

Johnny lost the coin toss. But his team, which had seemed tired before, exploded into action. The defense contained the Giants, who were forced to punt after failing to make first down.

The Colts began the drive from their own 20. Seven plays brought them to the New York 42. Johnny had a pass called for the next play. But he had seen the Giant middle linebacker drop back out of position to help his secondary defend against short passes.

It might be possible to open up that middle!

The view from the Giants' side as Alan Ameche starts through the hole. Johnny (19) is in the back, at right.

Johnny called a "trap" play on the line of scrimmage. His center blocked the Giant right tackle, Roosevelt Grier. His right guard brush-blocked the powerful Giant left tackle, Dick Modzelewski, letting him get through to be trapped by Colt left guard Art Spinney. With the middle cleared out, Alan the Horse went roaring through. The deep-lurking linebacker, Sam Huff, was bumped out of the way by the Colt right tackle. And Ameche was clear for a 23-yard gain.

Later, Ameche goes down after gaining only a yard. On top of him, with feet in the air, is the Giants' Sam Huff. The two other tacklers are Jim Patton *(20)* and Carl Karilivacz.

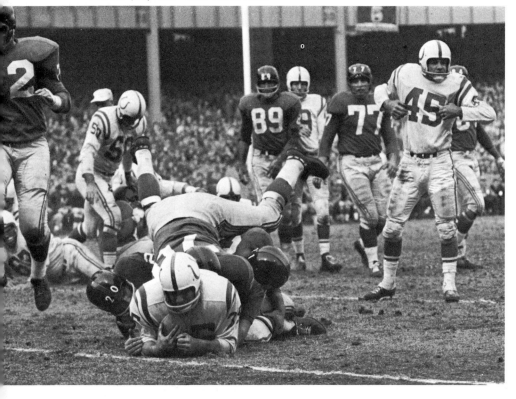

Alan Ameche, invisible in the pile, scores the winning touchdown in the 1958 championship game. His work done, Johnny *(far right)* walks off the field as the fans go wild with joy.

After a no-gain ground play, Johnny passed again to Berry. Now they were on the 8-yard line, first down and goal to go.

The coach told them, "Run three times, then try for a field goal." It was just what the Giants expected them to do.

On the first play, they sent Alan Ameche over right guard and gained only a yard. Then Johnny gambled. The Giant line was solid. So he sent a flat pass to end Jim Mutscheller, who caught it on the one-yard line and fell out of bounds.

On the next play, Alan the Horse crashed through the line.

Baltimore had won, 23-17. Weeb Ewbank never questioned Johnny's disobeying his order about staying on the ground. But others asked, "Why did you risk a pass that could have been intercepted?"

Johnny answered, "When you know what you're doing, they're not intercepted."

Confidence was the name of his game. He became famous as the best of the "stand-up" quarterbacks. Protected by a pocket of husky blockers, he would hang onto the ball as long as possible to let his receivers get downfield.

Johnny in his "pocket"

Johnny *(19)* cocks his arm for a pass during the second quarter of the 1959 championship game against the New York Giants. The Colts won, 31-16.

Johnny himself scores a touchdown in the 1959 championship game. Lenny Moore *(24)* sits on the ground after blocking a Giant defender. Jim Katcavage *(75)* and Dick Modzelewski *(77)* trail Johnny into the end zone.

The long pass was his trademark. But he could throw short, too. And whether a bomb or a lob, his passes usually went where they were sent.

Johnny was known for his ability to surprise his opponents with plays they had not expected. He was quick to spot weaknesses and exploit them with "automatics."

The Colts won the championship again in 1959. Johnny was voted Player of the Year. He threw touchdown passes in 47 consecutive games from 1956 to 1960, an all-time record.

During the following years, Johnny was as good as ever. But the Colts' running and blocking went downhill. In 1963, with a new coach named Don Shula, the team was reborn. From 1964 on, they were always first or second in their division.

Now the big prize became the Super Bowl.

End Lou Michaels *(left)*, famed for kicking field goals, talks with Johnny and Coach Don Shula before the 1967 title game.

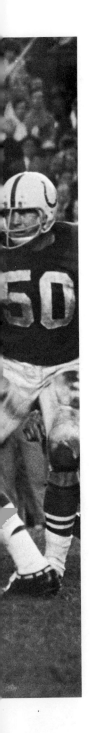

The Colts had their first chance at it in 1969. They faced the New York Jets, coached by the former Colt skipper, Weeb Ewbank.

Johnny had injured his elbow, so Earl Morrall started as quarterback. Three interceptions in the first half left the team scoreless to the Jets' 7.

In the third quarter, the Jets got two field goals and the score was 13-0. Sore elbow or not, Johnny went in. He got the ball moving. But the hustling Jets and their quarterback, Joe Namath, kept the Colts to a single touchdown and point-after.

Johnny hadn't been able to save them, as he had done so often. The Colts lost Super Bowl III, 16-7.

Despite a sore elbow, Johnny gets the ball moving during Super Bowl III. Other Colts are Dan Sullivan (71) and Bill Curry (50). Defending Jets are Gerry Philbin (81) and Paul Rochester (72).

Under a new coach, Don McCafferty, the Colts were second in 1969. They shaped up well in 1970, despite injuries, and had another crack at the Super Bowl.

Super Bowl V, the "Sandlot Super Bowl," was a strange game. Both the Colts and the Dallas Cowboys seemed to make mistake after mistake. The Cowboys scored with two field goals. Then Johnny threw a 75-yard pass that was tipped by one receiver, got away from a Dallas defensive back, and finally found a home with Colt end John Mackey. He went for a touchdown.

Late in the second quarter, Johnny was getting off a pass. A Dallas lineman smashed him, injuring his ribs. Johnny went out of the game.

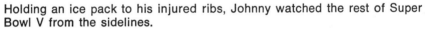

Holding an ice pack to his injured ribs, Johnny watched the rest of Super Bowl V from the sidelines.

Now it was Morrall's turn to go in for Johnny. The score was 13-6 in the last quarter, with the Cowboys on top. Texas fans screamed in dismay as the Colts took over through interceptions. A few minutes later, a touchdown and point conversion tied the score.

Five seconds were left when a rookie kicker, Jim O'Brien, made a 32-yard field goal. The Colts won, 16-13. The Vince Lombardi Super Bowl Trophy was theirs. And no Colt was happier than Johnny.

Someone asked, "Were you disappointed at not being in on the finish?"

"Not me. Football is a team game or it's nothing," said Johnny Unitas.

Johnny Unitas of the Baltimore Colts

JOHN UNITAS

He was born in Pittsburgh, Pennsylvania, on May 7, 1933. His father, of Lithuanian descent, died when Johnny was six. His widowed mother supported Johnny, his brother and two sisters.

Johnny graduated from St. Justin's High in 1951. It was here that he met the girl who would become his future wife, Dorothy Hoelle. All through the early, difficult years—and through the years of success, too—Dorothy has been at Johnny's side, helping him and encouraging him. They have five children.

Johnny has remained with the Baltimore Colts for 15 years. Highly respected by teammates and opposition alike, he is probably the outstanding "stand-up" quarterback of all time. He has written about his life in *Pro Quarterback: My Own Story* (1965); and about his game in *Playing Pro Football To Win* (1968).

RECORDS

Most touchdown passes, lifetime: 280
Most passes completed, lifetime: 2,616
Most yards gained passing, lifetime: 37,715
Most passes attempted, lifetime: 4,777
Most consecutive games with touchdown passes: 47

Jim Thorpe Award (Most Valuable Player)
1957
1967

All-League Selection: 1958, 1959, 1964, 1965, 1967